The Missing Lynx

Finally, A Speak-In-Public Learning
System For High School Students

Other Books By Stephen M. Gower, CSP

Celebrate The Butterflies
Presenting With Confidence In Public

Think Like A Giraffe
*A Reach For The Sky Guide In Creativity And
Maximum Performance*

What Do They See When They See You Coming?
The Power Of Perception Over Reality

Like A Pelican In The Desert
Leadership Redefined: Beyond Awkwardness

Zebra Dazzle
How To Build Stunning Teams

Have You Encouraged Someone Today?
366 Ways To Practice Encouragement

Upsize Selling
Increase Your Sales With The Mix Of Six

The Focus Crisis
Nurturing Focus Within A Culture Of Change

The Art Of Killing Kudzu
Management By Encouragement

The Missing Lynx

Finally, A Speak-In-Public Learning System For
High School Students

It Is Easier Than You Think!

Stephen M. Gower

Certified Speaking Professional

Lectern Publishing
P. O. Box 1065, Toccoa, GA, 30577

First edition, published in 1998 by LECTERN PUBLISHING, P.O. Box 1065, Toccoa, GA 30577.

Sixth Printing, 2007

Library of Congress Catalog Card No.: 98-94138
ISBN: 1-880150-79-4

With Mom In Mind

She claims she never taught me. But she did teach hundreds of my friends. Monday through Friday, during after-school hours, mother would teach public speaking skills to very young students in the living room of our home. At the time, I did not value the importance of what she was doing. Now, I recognize that she was making a huge difference in the lives of her students.

At this moment, I am thinking of one of her students who became Star Student of his entire state. He later earned graduate degrees in both law and medicine. His father once told me that much of his son's success had to do with the confidence that found his son because he took speech lessons from my mother.

To this day, I have known no one else who did what mother did – give private speech lessons in her home for young students.

I cannot become my mother. I do hope to duplicate in some fashion within you what she did for so many. I do hope to present the speak-in-public challenge in such a way that you will choose to say – "I can do this!"

Acknowledgements

For more than a quarter of a century, I have reminded students or business professionals of this reality — "You are a composite, a mixture, of your 'where you have been.'"

As I prepare the manuscript for this book, I sense the power of that statement as it applies to my own life. I write this book with a wonderful peace and an awesome confidence. Both the peace and confidence are possible because of my "where I have been." I hereby acknowledge all of those persons who have contributed to my "where I have been" and have blessed me beyond measure.

The peace and confidence that accompany me in this writing-journey have unfolded because I have been the beneficiary of a significant, educational experience and a tremendous amount of encouragement.

I easily acknowledge the influence of my family, my teachers, my students, my fellow members in the National Speakers Association – and of course of my Heavenly Father. Thank you all. From the bottom of my heart, thank you all!

Special appreciation should be extended to Emily Adams. Few are as "in tune with" high school students and the "written word" as Emily. Her perspective, her suggestions, and her encouragement contributed significantly to this book.

Once again, our director of operations, Amy Camp, has been a driving force behind an extremely important project. Every professional speaker and author should have an "Amy."

I must acknowledge the support of my wife. Lynne, I have seen you weep and I have seen you laugh as I spoke. You have cared enough to confront — and you have been the queen of encouragement. You have consistently reminded me that this is what God wants me to do — I believe you are correct. Thanks for all you do — and for who you are!

Mission Statement

The mission of *The Missing Lynx* is to provide high school students with a speak-in-public learning system that is educational, exciting, and encouraging.

Contents

An Introduction

Now Stephen "do your homework. And, when you finish, go have some fun. For the next two hours, I will be teaching in the living room."

For close to ten years, my mother said those words to me. Mother did not tutor English or math. She did not teach piano or the violin. In our living room, mother taught public speaking to elementary, middle school, and high school students. To this day, I hear about the huge difference that she made in their lives. To this day, I have never heard of anyone else doing precisely what she did.

Well, you and I are not literally with each other right now, but I want you to feel as if we are. My hope is that I can bring to you just a portion of the knowledge my mother brought to hundreds of boys and girls – and young men and women.

I attempted to do that when I taught public speaking on the college level as an adjunct professor for more than a decade. And, perhaps even more importantly, I have presented more than four thousand speeches – enabling me to transform theory into practice. It is my hope that this book will enable you to benefit from both my teaching and my "out-there-speaking" experiences.

This book is precisely for you. Its goal is simple – to share with you this concept – SPEAKING IN PUBLIC IS EASIER THAN YOU THINK. You should have been told this much earlier. Many of you were not. You should have received basic "speaking-in-public" skills earlier. Many of you did not.

The past is behind you. It no longer has to control you. It is up to you. You can now choose to learn for yourself that speaking in public is indeed easier than you once thought.

An Introduction

This book is designed to help you move beyond any symptoms of frustration to a specific public-speaking-system – The Lynx System. You will later learn why I refer to this system as the "LYNX" system as opposed to the "links." For now, let me assure you that this is by intent – not by accident.

This book is written to help you fill in the gap – to find *The Missing Lynx* – to learn how to speak with confidence in public. This system is easier than you might have ever imagined. The Lynx System is light – not heavy!

The Missing Lynx – Finally, A Speak-In-Public Learning System For High School Students is divided into five parts. The five basic parts of this book are:

1) The Lost Lynx
2) The Lynx Lessons
3) The Lynx Logic
4) The Lynx List
5) The Lasting Lynx.

Part One, The Lost Lynx, will remind you that, for the most part, we as a society have failed to do two things. In the first place, we have failed to persuade you that your ability to speak in public should be vitally important to you. We have not convinced you that the one who speaks in public well can position himself or herself miles ahead of the competition. In the second place, we have failed to teach you how to speak in public.

We have left out something very important – *The Missing Lynx* – an emphasis on speaking with confidence in public. To a large degree, emphasis on the skill has become lost. In thousands of high schools, most everything imaginable is being taught – except for The Lost Lynx – *The Missing Lynx* – the skill to speak with confidence in public. Part One addresses this void.

Section Two, The Lynx Lessons, will share vital foundation pieces that must mold your new approach to the entire concept of presenting with confidence in public. You may well choose to read and re-read these lessons, as they will prove vital to your growth.

Basically, The Lynx Lessons are shared to service your thought-life about speaking in public. When it comes to speaking in front of others, it is what you think about, and what you do not think about, that influences both your attitude about speaking and the effectiveness of your speaking.

An Introduction

Accordingly, please place these Lynx Lessons into the center of your mind-tank.

Part Three, The Lynx Logic, is certainly the core of *The Missing Lynx*. It builds upon the traditional definition of lynx as "a small, wild cat with relatively long legs, thick fur, and tufted ears – particularly respected as being keen-sighted." (Here, "keen" means sharp, or astute, or intent, or bright.) When one person wants to compliment another on his or her understanding, grasp, vision, or perception, that person may choose to say – "You are lynx-eyed," or "lynx-like," or "keen-sighted," or "sharp-sighted."

Throughout this book, the term "lynx" will build upon the concept that the lynx cat is known for being both light and bright.

When I refer to The Lynx Speak-In-Public Learning System, I refer to a system that asks you to be keen-sighted. I want you to see clearly. And again, this is what I want you to see clearly – SPEAKING WITH CONFIDENCE IN PUBLIC IS MUCH EASIER THAN YOU THINK.

Please read these next few sentences very carefully. Study them again and again. The lynx cat is primarily nocturnal. Most of its activity takes place at night. That is when its keen vision, its sharp-sightedness, works to its advantage.

When you have a speech approaching, when you feel darkness around you, when you become exceptionally nervous, do not become discouraged. This can become the moment when you begin to shine. When others are overcome with "fear of the night," you can apply this light (not heavy) system. When others are blinded in the night, you can be bright, you can see clearly, you can be keen-sighted. You can be lynx-eyed.

I am going to show you how to do this. You can indeed become sharp-sighted the night before you speak – and the night when you speak.

The Lynx Logic, Part Number Three, explains my reasoning. It shares the basic fundamentals of writing and presenting speeches that equal the rationale behind The Lynx System. It states that writing and presenting speeches is as simple as C, C , C, and C:

1) The Content
2) The Construction
3) The Carrying
4) The Connection.

Much of our time together will be spent exploring these Four Cs. The Lynx Logic presents the central reasoning, rationale, or thinking behind The Lynx Speak-In-Public Learning System For High School Students.

Part Number Four, The Lynx List, recognizes that there will be times when you will appreciate a quick-glance into The Lynx Speak-In-Public Learning System For High School Students. Accordingly, it presents a reminder list that very briefly touches upon some of the key points of our system. We will refer to The Lynx List as a Top 20 List.

Let me caution you here. The few pages that comprise The Lynx List should never replace the whole book. The keys here are "reference" and "reminder," not "replacement."

Part Five, The Lasting Lynx, is brief in content. However, the message it presents is very significant. Once you begin learning this system, it can become something that can literally serve you the rest of your life. Part Five will emphasize to you that The Lynx System lasts. It can make a tremendous difference for a lifetime. It can equal ADVANTAGE SPEAKER for a lifetime.

Before I conclude this introduction, let me state to you that I am the author of *Celebrate The*

THE MISSING LYNX

Butterflies – Presenting With Confidence In Public.
Although it is basically the course that I taught on the college level, and although business professionals across the country have purchased it as a "how-to" tool, I believe you may find it helpful. When I feel the benefit to you might be especially meaningful, I will cross reference to *Celebrate The Butterflies* with specific page listings. (Your school library may have a copy of *Celebrate The Butterflies* – ISBN number 1-880150-73-5. Or, you may purchase it through any bookstore if you desire.)

In the preceding pages, I have shared with you the basic, five-part structure of *The Missing Lynx*: The Lost Lynx, The Lynx Lessons, The Lynx Logic, The Lynx List, and The Lasting Lynx. Now, let us discover just how easy this can be. And, remember, as mama used to say, "Do your homework – then you can have some fun."

Part One

The Lost Lynx

CHAPTER 1

Our Bad

We have not been treating you fairly. Our educational system, and our society as a whole, have been supposedly preparing you for high school graduation, and for life's challenges, without addressing an issue that is absolutely crucial to your future – and to your present. Unfortunately, for most of you, it is a major missing link in your education. For those of us responsible for providing you with essential tools for your growth, it is a major mistake on our part.

THE MISSING LYNX

We have deprived you of instruction and encouragement in a crucial skill. We have denied you the satisfaction and fulfillment that occurs when you develop and express this skill. By our very omission of emphasis, we have said to you, "It is not important for you to learn to speak with confidence in public – nor is it important for you to focus on fundamental skills in communication." This has been OUR BAD.

Certainly, there are some exceptions involved here. A few school systems, select teachers, and even some families have sought to equip their students and their sons and daughters with at least the opportunity to acquire these speaking and communication skills. Unfortunately, some have refused to take advantage of the opportunities with which they were presented. However, in most instances, we have failed you. For the most part, we, the society that is counting on you to help lead us into the future, have said to you – "Look, your capacity to speak with confidence in public, your ability to communicate within a culture that literally spins on the axis of communication, is not important."

Oh, for sure we did not say – "It is not important"– not word by word. But sometimes, what you do not say – and what you do not do – are as important, if not more important – than what you do say – and what you do.

The truth is this – few of us have said anything, or done anything, to indicate to you how important these speaking skills are in today's society. If we are waiting on colleges, vocational schools, the workforce, or communities at large to help you here, we are only fooling ourselves – and we are certainly doing you an injustice. Again, it is OUR BAD! For the most part, we LOST THE LYNX. We left out something crucial. It is *The Missing Lynx* – the "speak-in-public" skills that you so desperately need. For far too long, we have been waiting "far too long" to assist you in acquiring these speaking and communication skills.

I have often wondered what our reluctance to address these vital "speaking skills" has been saying to you. Does our reluctance say – "These speaking skills are not important"? Does our reluctance say – "These speaking skills are so difficult that someone else must address them at a later date"? Does our reluctance say – "This is something you should already know how to do"?

What They Are – What They Are Not – What You Must Do

Let me state this emphatically. These "speaking skills" ARE vitally important! They ARE NOT difficult – speaking in public is amazingly easier than you think.

This skills-set equals that which you MUST consciously seek to acquire and nurture. My point is this – we should have been telling you this all along. By what we should have done even before you entered kindergarten, by what we should have done while you were in grades one through eight, by what we should have done during your after-school hours, we should have been screaming – "Look, these speaking skills are crucial." We should have been telling you – "The sooner you learn them, the better – the more you nurture them, the better." We goofed. In many cases, we simply let you down. And, we confused you.

We Confused You

We have not stressed speaking skills! Before you entered the first grade, you had perhaps already been exposed to one or more of the following: snow skiing, swimming, ballet, karate, baseball, boxing, piano, basketball, dancing, violin, singing, soccer, guitar, or hockey. Now, I certainly do not mean to indicate that there is anything wrong with the before-mentioned. I just want to bring attention to what has not been emphasized – speaking skills.

Before you entered high school, you had already been exposed to one or more of the following: little league, band, cheerleading, junior varsity sports, advanced piano, dance, karate, or snowboarding. Again, nothing is wrong with stressing the before-mentioned. I just want to bring attention to what has not been emphasized – speaking skills. Surely we confused you.

Enough About The Past

Well, that is enough about the past. We do not need to dwell on that anymore. Let us now address your future. You can take this to the bank – you will be asked to speak again – and again – and again. You will be asked to talk to groups at work, to speak to certain organizations, to give sales presentations, to present in court – or in church – or in front of your team.

Here is something else you can take to the bank – you can learn to present yourself and your thoughts with clarity and with conviction! It is not a matter of simply wishing. It can actually happen.

However, speaking of wishing, may I share some wishes with you? I wish I had possessed a book like this when I was your age. I wish I had written it much earlier in my life. Finally, I wish, or hope, that it will help remedy OUR BAD.

Chapter Summary

- Speaking skills are vital.
- Speaking skills are not difficult.
- The speaking-skills set must be acquired and nurtured.
- We should have told you this sooner.

Part Two

The Lynx
Lessons

CHAPTER 2

You Can Do This

I t is easier than you think – much easier than you think.

One of the most important skills you will need if you want to succeed in school, work, and life is the ability to speak and communicate with confidence in public. And, the exciting thing is this – this is something you can do.

This book will help you – if you allow it to help you. I do not want you to read this book because you have to read it. I understand that, in many cases, it is becoming required reading. But, I prefer that you read, study, enjoy, and constantly refer to it because you choose to – not because you have to. Learning from this book should be a challenge – not a chore. Keep it a choice – and, YOU CAN DO THIS. Let it become a chore – you will be up against the wall.

Whatever your goal in life, *The Missing Lynx – Finally, A Speak-In-Public Learning System For High School Students* can help you. The capacity to communicate is central in our society. It is crucial. But, it is not complicated. You can do this. The key is in YOUR THOUGHTS.

Chapter Summary

- Speaking in public is easier than you think.
- You can do this.
- The key is in your thoughts.

CHAPTER 3

You Are A Thought Maker

What do you say to yourself? It is simple. The thoughts you have – ultimately the thoughts you keep – eventually determine whether or not "you can do this." Before you and I can form thoughts for an expression, we must first form thoughts about the expressing, thoughts about the talking, thoughts about the presenting. Thoughts themselves can keep us from speaking, or they can encourage us to speak. What you say to yourself and about yourself is CRUCIAL.

THE MISSING LYNX

Accordingly, for a brief while here, I want to address the thoughts you may be having about speaking in public. There is an important distinction here. At this point I am not addressing the thoughts you might share with a friend, one-to-one, or the thoughts you might share with hundreds of people. Here, I am only addressing thoughts that you share with yourself – thoughts that relate to self-talk.

SELF-TALK THOUGHTS are in many ways the most important thoughts you ever make. Self-talk thoughts impact your confidence. Self-talk thoughts affect your clarity. They even make you tired or energetic. Self-talk thoughts make you say yes or no – "Yes, I can speak in public" – "No, I can not speak in public."

When I taught public speaking, many of my students did not understand that they were making thoughts about themselves as speakers, and that these thoughts had a tremendous amount of power over them. Accordingly, they should have chosen their breed of thoughts carefully. They did not. The very thoughts they made about themselves as speakers tended to influence their progress in the course. And, in many cases, the influence was not good.

Choose Your Thoughts Carefully

Quite simply, there are negative thoughts and there are positive thoughts. The negative thoughts equal Torture Thoughts. The positive thoughts equal Triumph Thoughts. Negative or positive, you make your own thoughts!

Torture Thoughts, negative thoughts, equal a list that includes the following: "No" . . . "Not me" . . . "Not now" . . . "Never" . . . "I cannot do that; what would I say?" . . . "I might not make sense; they will laugh at me."

Triumph Thoughts, positive thoughts, equal a list that includes the following: "Sure" . . . "Yes, I can do that" . . . "What is there to lose?" . . . "I will need this later, why not learn how to do it now" . . . "I can do this."

Now, please hear me clearly here – if you are like me, you will always have both positive thoughts and negative thoughts. If you follow the system I teach here, your negative thoughts may well be reduced in number, but elimination of negative thoughts is not the goal here. Your goal is to become concerned with what you do with your negative thoughts. Eventually, the number of your negative thoughts should actually diminish. But they will never totally evaporate.

In similar fashion, I encourage you to examine what you do with your positive thoughts. I would hope that you would hold on to these thoughts so that they can continue to serve you well.

The thoughts you make can lead to solutions, growth, success, and satisfaction. The thoughts you make can also deny you solutions, growth, success, and satisfaction. Yes, you are indeed a thought maker. Choose the thoughts you make with great care.

Chapter Summary

- You make your own thoughts.
- What you say to yourself and about yourself is crucial.
- Self-talk thoughts impact your confidence.
- Choose your thoughts carefully.

CHAPTER 4

Where Do Your Thoughts Go?

Ultimately, your thoughts about public speaking and communication should go into one of two places. There are no other places that the thoughts you make about speaking in public can go. Please remember this throughout high school – THE THOUGHTS YOU MAKE SHOULD HEAD TOWARD ONE OF TWO PLACES. Who decides which of these two places will eventually hold a particular thought? YOU DO!

That is correct. You make the thought. You determine where the thought goes.

It Is Quite Simple

You are the one person who determines the thoughts that you have about whether or not you can speak with confidence in public. Furthermore, after you do make those thoughts, you determine what happens to them. All of the thoughts that you make about speaking with confidence in public should go into one of two places – The Waste-Thought Basket or The Trophy-Thought Case.

The Waste-Thought Basket

When you have negative thoughts about speaking and communicating with confidence in public – and you will – place them into the WASTE-THOUGHT BASKET. Get rid of them. Throw those thoughts away. You have the power to throw them away. Do it!

Many years ago, while I was in high school, I worked after school as a radio announcer. In those days, our music was not on eight tracks or CDs – it was on records – the old fashioned vinyls. A needle would move from point to point playing the music. On many occasions, the needle would get stuck. The same thing would play over again and again.

Never let the needle get stuck on your negative thoughts! Stop playing them over in your mind again and again. You make your thoughts – you determine where they go – you can place your negative thoughts into the Waste-Thought Basket.

The thoughts that inappropriately hold you back – those thoughts that zap your confidence and bite your spirit – have a special place. That special place is the trash can. These thoughts are garbage. Throw them out. Do not hold on to them. You are the announcer-in-charge here. Stop your negative self-talk. When negative self-talk does happen, place your Torture Thoughts into the Waste-Thought Basket.

If you are a cheerleader, you know better than to say – "I can not jump. I have no spirit. I can not lead. I can not set the example." You know better than to torture yourself like that. If you are an offensive end, you know better than to say – "I can never catch a ball. I am too clumsy. I can never be fast enough to outrun him." You know better than to say to yourself, "Our quarterback is no good. He does not like me. And, if he ever threw to me, he would not want me to catch the ball."

You know better than to talk to yourself like this. Why? Because it is negative! Negative!! Negative!!! It is Torture Talk. And, it is no good.

If you are studying for a big test, you know better than to say to yourself, "Study does not help you learn. This is not going to do any good. I will just stop it. It is hopeless."

The cheerleader, the offensive end, and the student know to throw negative, Torture Thoughts into the Waste-Thought Basket. So does the confident high school communicator and speaker. Negative thoughts do torture us. They hurt us. But, they cannot do anything to us if we get rid of them – if we place them where they belong – into the Waste-Thought Basket.

The Trophy-Thought Case

The high school student who learns to speak with confidence in public knows what to do with the negative (no), self-defeating thoughts. He, or she, knows to get rid of them – to place them into the Waste-Thought Basket. He, or she, also knows what

Where Do Your Thoughts Go?

to do with the positive (yes), self-asserting thoughts. He, or she, knows how to hold on to them, to put them on display in a TROPHY-THOUGHT CASE – to "keep them around" so they can be viewed and helpful in a persistent fashion.

Please hear me at this point. You are responsible for your thoughts. And, when you have good thoughts, you should hold on to them. Put them on display in a Trophy-Thought Case. Write your positive thoughts about speaking in public down on paper. The exercises that follow will help you protect your positive thoughts. You can triumph over negativity. And when you do – record it. It is smart to remind yourself of prior instances when you thought well – and when you did well.

Again, please hear me correctly here. At this point in your life, your Trophy-Thought Case is not built to hold copies or recordings of your great speeches. What I want you to learn to put on display, within the very core of your thinking, is this – you will have positive thoughts – they will normally not occur as big events – they will normally occur as little steps. So what I want you to learn to do is this – LEARN TO CELEBRATE INCREMENTAL FINISHEDNESS.

Celebrate Small Steps – Little, Positive Thoughts

Learn to place your little, positive thoughts into your Trophy-Thought Case. Little, positive thoughts create big, positive thoughts. Little, positive thoughts eventually create confident speakers. Value your Trophy-Thought Case.

Chapter Summary

- You determine where your thoughts go.
- Negative thoughts belong in the Waste-Thought Basket.
- Positive thoughts belong in the Trophy-Thought Case.

CHAPTER 5

Who Do They Think They Are?

nd, who do you think they are?

For the past several pages, I have been making a case for the fact that you are responsible for your thoughts. You create your own Thought-Life.

However, I well remember how I used to feel as a high school student. In fact, I still allow others to have more control over my personal feelings than I should allow them to have. But, both you and I should understand this – when another person causes us to feel bad, or afraid, or like "I just cannot speak in public," this is occurring in part because we are allowing someone else to have control over our feelings. We all need to work on this one.

Let me recount for you an experience that happened to me almost twenty years ago when I was teaching public speaking. It was mid-quarter. One of my students approached me and said that she could not give her second speech. I asked her, "Why not?" She responded, "Because you intimidate me."

I apologized to her for anything I had done to hurt her feelings. I also suggested to her that she might want to look again at precisely why she felt intimidated. Ultimately, we both agreed that she had to take some responsibility for her feelings. (By the way, she gave speech number two – and speech number three – and earned an A in the course.)

You may think that they will talk bad about you if you make a mistake in your speech. I doubt it. I doubt that they will even think that much about you after you make your speech. But if they do – if they do think about your mistake – do they think they are important enough to make you feel bad about yourself? I think not.

Who Do They Think They Are?

I know not – as long as you choose not to let it happen. The real question is this one – "Do you think they are important enough to make you feel bad about yourself?" It is who you think they are – not who they think they are – that forms your thought-life. And, ultimately, it is who you think you are that matters the most!

They cannot make you feel bad about yourself – unless you cooperate with them.

Chapter Summary

- "Who they think you are" is not as important as "who you think you are."
- They cannot make you feel bad about yourself unless you cooperate with them.

CHAPTER 6

Do I Have A Surprise For You

I f you hold the record for the most rushing yardage for your high school, if you are considering playing intramural football, and someone says – "You don't know how to run with the football," are you going to listen? Of course not.

If you have been elected freshman class president, sophomore class president, junior class president, if you are now running for senior class president, and someone says, "You can never win an election," are you going to listen? Of course not.

If you have played the trumpet ever since the sixth grade, if your band director assigns you first chair in the high school band, and if someone says, "You don't even know how to play the trumpet," are you going to listen? Of course not.

If you have taken classes in computers for five years, if you actually run the computer department for a large retail establishment, and if someone says, "You can't even turn on a computer," are you going to listen? Of course not.

Here is the surprise I have for you – IT IS NO DIFFERENT IN SPEAKING. And, so to speak, you already have the passing yardage, you already have won the elections, you already know how to play the horn, you already know how to master the computer.

Your life has prepared you to speak and communicate in public. The surprise I have for you is this – your "WHERE YOU HAVE BEEN" – whatever that is – has qualified you to become a confident speaker. You may not know it – you probably do not know it – but, my friend, you are already experienced.

Do I Have A Surprise For You

You Have Already Paid Your Dues

You do not merely study history. You have a history. Your history is a mixture of who you are from the inside – your FROM WITHIN, and who you are from the outside – your FROM WITHOUT. You have given skills and acquired skills. You have had your own experiences – you have observed and studied the experiences of others.

You have made music – been moved by music. You have created problems – solved problems. You have structured twigs – arranged marbles. You have thrown and caught balls and batons. You have experience at creating, at structuring, at arranging, at giving, and at receiving.

If speech is life – and it is, if speaking is living – and it is, then you have been speaking for the whole of your life. You are ready for this book. Nobody, nothing can take that away from you. You have already paid your dues. Once you really understand this, then you are free to discover something else.

The Gift Is Inside

Part of the surprise I have for you is this –
YOU HAVE A BIG GIFT INSIDE YOU.

Over the last many years, both high school and college students have indicated to me that I have given them a tremendous gift. If I understand them correctly, they are attempting to thank me for helping them learn how to speak in public. They have been giving me a lot of credit – too much credit. I accept and appreciate their point. But, in a way, they are wrong.

I did not really give them a gift. What I actually did was help them discover a gift – a gift they already had. What I really did was help them see, unleash, and sculpt the gift that was already there.

What I helped them do, and what I hope to help you do, touches the issue of camouflage-removal.

Remove The Camouflage

I am afraid that you are unaware of the gift within you. I am afraid that you have a track record that equals many years of gift-blockage. Perhaps you have blocked out the gift of expressing yourself so effectively that you no longer see that gift. But, that does not mean that it is no longer there.

It is possible that you have placed upon yourself layer after layer of negative thoughts – Torture Thoughts. You have refused to place these Torture Thoughts into the Waste-Thought Basket. Perhaps, you have allowed these negative thoughts to accumulate too much – so much that they now equal a suit of camouflage. Perhaps you no longer see the massive gift of experience, excitement, and expression that is within you. What was once close to the surface is now deep below. Perhaps, you have fooled yourself into thinking that you have nothing to offer. Stop fooling yourself. It is time to celebrate yourself. This may come as a surprise to you, but the gift is there. Remove the camouflage!

Enough

Ideas, instincts, inspirations – each initially may be positioned very close to the surface that equals your person.

Your negative self-talk and all of its support form some sort of cataracts – or blinders – or camouflage – over your ideas, instincts, and inspirations.

Hopefully, you reach a point during your high school education where you recognize what is happening to you – the gift within you has gone into deep hiding. Not only do you recognize the situation, you choose to do something about it.

You shout ENOUGH! You are going to take a crucial step to help you become who you know you can be. You are not going to be molded by what everyone else is doing – or by what everyone else is not doing. You are going to do it differently. You are going to do it your best way. And, the surprise I have for you at this point is this – "You can do it your best way."

Stick With It

Building upon the gift, or surprise, that is already within you, you are going to be smart enough to build a speak-in-public learning system that works – and you are going to be smart enough to stick with it.

Now, let me elaborate upon this "stick with it" point. You must choose to do precisely that. Why? Because there will be "ups and downs" for you here. Again, growth will never occur as single event. It will unfold as process – and there will be downs – dips – in the process. You will "travel by detour."

Caution – Practice
Does Not Make Perfect

At this writing, I have given more than four thousand speeches. I have never given a perfect presentation. I am not sure that is possible. No, practice does not make for perfect – but, PRACTICE DOES MAKE FOR BETTER.

The surprise I have for you is this – you can make progress as you repeatedly remind yourself that speaking with confidence in public is much easier than you ever thought. But, please remember this – practice is essential. For our purposes, practice equals preparation.

Bring Preparation To
Awkward Situations

Life is awkward. It is not predictable, nor fair – but it is gift, and it can be exceptionally meaningful.

You and confidence can meet each other – particularly within awkward situations such as speaking in front of your high school literature class – if, and only if, you pay the preparation price.

Confidence cannot be borrowed – or stolen – or bought. Confidence happens as a natural result of something else happening. Confidence can only come as a result of something else. It is the "effect" side of "cause and effect."

You Do Not Find Confidence – It Finds You

For years, I am afraid, you have been given the wrong impression – the idea that confidence is something you can find – you go out and look for it – you discover it – and you pick it up. This is not true. Confidence finds you – you do not find it.

My suggestion to you is this – quit looking for confidence. Confidence will most likely find you when you are looking for something else. Look for ways to practice your presentation – even as you remember that practice makes for better – not perfect. Look for ways to prepare – and prepare – and prepare!

Bring preparation to awkward situations. And, most likely, confidence will actually find you.

Do I Have A Surprise For You

Remember, no one else can give you confidence. I cannot give you confidence any more than I can motivate you. Incidentally, ultimately, the only kind of starter is a self-starter. You must choose to motivate yourself. You must choose to start building and nurturing your own speak-in-public skills. Once you make these correct choices, you position yourself so that confidence can notice you. Never forget this – confidence comes as the "end result" – after you have paid the preparation price.

Chapter Summary

- You already have experience.
- Your "where you have been" is a big plus.
- You have paid your dues.
- There is a gift inside you.
- Remove the camouflage.
- Stick with the system.
- Practice to improve – not to be perfect.
- Let confidence find you.

CHAPTER 7

Let The Fun Begin

Without appearing to brag, I want to share something with you. I am told that literally hundreds of students anticipated taking my college course in public speaking. Oh, for sure, there were also hundreds that dreaded and postponed the venture – but many anticipated our time together. To this day, now ten years hence, students still express appreciation for the experience.

Why the accolades? Why the success? Why the huge numbers? Why do high school students still call me to help them prepare for a special speech at graduation or a challenging presentation at a state organization?

They came to my classes, and they still call me now, because I know how to allow the learning process to be fun. I know how to make all of this "speak-in-public" stuff exciting – not boring, meaningful – not miserable, fun – not foolish. I know how to help students find *The Missing Lynx*. I know how to arrange for the release of the gift. I know how to encourage students to be their best selves and their best speakers. I know how to remind students that they are "ok" as they are. Basically, I do not ask students to change their personalities.

Your Style Is The Extension Of Your Personality

It remains within my head and heart to this day. I had just finished delivering my presentation on "speaking skills" to a state group of high school student-leaders.

Let The Fun Begin

Upon completion of my presentation, I asked those high school students if they had any questions for me, or if they would like to comment on what they found to be most meaningful in my presentation. From the front row, a young man raised his hand and said – "It is certainly a relief for me to know that I do not have to change my personality to be an effective speaker. I liked what you said about 'style' actually being an extension of my personality."

The fun begins, high school student, when you recognize that your audience wants you to be you. Anything that varies from you hints of phoniness or insincerity. The Lynx System encourages you to be yourself – and to have fun doing it. This truth seems to come as a refreshing shock to most high school students. Listen, please.

To speak is not to act. Speaking is, in many ways, as natural as breathing. Speaking in public is not a weird thing. It is a natural thing.

When someone asks you to speak, they are not asking you to be who you are not – they are asking you to express, or extend, who you are. Your speaking style is you – just as much as your walking style, or your jogging style, or your swimming style, or your clothing style is you.

The fun starts when you allow yourself to be yourself. When you do that, both you and your audience can find the experience meaningful. Your speaking style is not only up to you, YOUR SPEAKING STYLE IS YOU. Do not ever forget this.

Play With Words

We have taught you how to play with marbles and kites. We have taught you how to play with plastic toy pieces and tiny wooden logs. We have taught you how to play with footballs, basketballs, baseballs, ping pong balls, tennis balls, and soccer balls. But, we have not, for the most part, taught you how to play with words. We have deprived you.

When I say "let the fun begin," I invite you to play with words. When you learn the fundamental Lynx Speak-In-Public Learning System For High School Students, you learn the fun that travels along with playing with words.

I challenge you to have fun playing with words. Switch them around – couple them together – enhance one with several others. Build, tear down – build again. Go tell – go sell – go show – all with words. Paint mind-pictures with words – the setting sun, the strong defensive end, the honorable teacher, the outstanding band that you enjoyed last week.

Yes, to play with words is not silly at all – to play with words is the smart thing to do.

Your Nervous Energy Helps You

As I conclude this chapter, I want to remind you that there is a way for the very nervousness that you feel about speaking to equal an advantage – a fun advantage for you. The fun begins – and the fun continues – when you discover two things. In the first place, when you look at speaking in public as a fun thing, your nervousness can work for you rather than against you. In the second place, when you look upon speaking in public as a fun thing, you discover that presenting with confidence in public is much easier than you ever imagined.

The Lynx System shows you how your nervousness can work for you. (The key here equals PREPARATION.) The Lynx System also illustrates how EASY this can be. (The keys here equal your THOUGHT-LIFE and your STYLE – the ability to enjoy being yourself.)

THE MISSING LYNX

Chapter Summary

- The Lynx System is fun.
- Have fun being yourself.
- Style is the extension of your personality.
- Your speaking style is YOU.
- Play with words – and have fun doing it!

Part Three
The Lynx Logic

CHAPTER 8

As Easy As C, C, C And C

ou will discover *The Missing Lynx* when you understand that speaking in public is as easy as C, C, C, and C. You must understand:
1) The CONTENT
2) The CONSTRUCTION
3) The CARRYING
4) The CONNECTION.

The Lynx Speaking System says that the sizzling speaking skills all relate to The Content, The Construction, The Carrying, and The Connection.

To understand the importance of The Content, you must be a "QUESTIONEER." To understand the importance of The Construction, you must be an "ENGINEER." To understand the importance of The Carrying, you must be a "TRANSPORTER." To understand the importance of The Connection, you must be an "IMPACTER."

Why should speaking in public be easier than you might have thought? Because you already know how to be a "questioneer." Because you already know how to be an "engineer." Because you already know how to be a "transporter." Because you already know how to be an "impacter."

You already have the "necessary stuff."

Chapter Summary

- Speaking in public is an easy as C, C, C, and C.
- Focus on The Content, The Construction, The Carrying, and The Connection.
- Be a "Questioneer," "Engineer," "Transporter," and "Impacter."

CHAPTER 9

The Content

Be A "Questioneer"

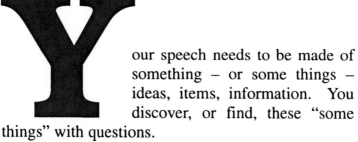our speech needs to be made of something – or some things – ideas, items, information. You discover, or find, these "some things" with questions.

This should make you feel great – because you have been good with questions for the whole of your life. Now, some of your questions may have been answered for you by the very nature of any assigned speech you may have been given. Nevertheless, there are several key questions out there – questions to be answered by your teacher – or most probably by you. The questions you ask provide The CONTENT you need to CONSTRUCT the speech you want to CARRY from yourself to another person.

There are four kinds of questions you must ask as you begin to form the content, or the makeup, of your speech. You ask:

1) PURPOSE-QUESTIONS
2) PERSON-QUESTIONS
3) PLACE-QUESTIONS
4) PROCESS-QUESTIONS.

The very questions you ask, and the answers you provide, both from within and out from yourself, help you meet the first leg of the 4C challenge – The Content.

Ask Purpose-Questions

You ask – "Am I trying to SHOW, TELL, or SELL?"

In a "Show" speech, you "put on a show." Your purpose is to entertain the audience. If you are effective, they enjoy. If you are ineffective, they endure. What should you expect in the "Show" speech? Your simple purpose is to expect them to feel entertained.

In a "Tell" speech, you simply have a story to tell. You want to inform your audience about a place, or a person, or a process, or a philosophy. You have no precise expectations of your audience – other than the fact that you do expect them to listen, and you do want them to feel informed.

In a "Sell" speech, your purpose is actually two-fold. You want your audience to feel a certain way – and to do a certain thing. Please note this – your purpose is not necessarily to change their minds – nor is it your purpose necessarily to change their behavior. They may already be thinking and behaving in just the fashion that your speech suggests. If they are not thinking, and acting, as your speech suggests, then your purpose is to "sell" them on both an attitude and a behavior.

Worded another way, in the "Sell" speech you want to persuade them to discover, or rediscover, a certain feeling about a particular subject. But remember, your purpose here is not merely to call for a feeling – you want to persuade them to act – to do something.

The Lynx Speak-In-Public Learning System For High School Students says – "You must know the PURPOSE of your speech." At this point, let me add two side-bar statements. In the first place, while you are in high school, it is quite possible that your teacher will determine the purpose of your speech. In the second place, your teacher may instruct you to deliver a type of speech that I do not specifically address in this book. Many will choose to refer to that type of speech as a "demonstration" speech. Although it is not our purpose to specifically address this type of speech, I do want to suggest that a blended modification of the "Show," "Tell," and "Sell" speech types might be useful for you.

Fundamentally, however, your purpose-questions will often find their answers in places that look like the "Show," or "Tell," or "Sell." (Helpful reading in the area of the purpose of a speech can be found in *Celebrate The Butterflies*, pages 43-46.)

Ask Person-Questions

It is simple – but oh, so serious. You must know as much as possible about your AUDIENCE. Naturally, if you are speaking to your high school class, many of your questions will already be answered.

But, what if you are speaking for Kiwanis, or for church? What if you are presenting in court, or talking to the Little League team that you coach? What if you are presenting a sales proposal before a particular committee? In each of these cases, you must be able to answer basic questions about your audiences' age, education, expectations, bias or opinions, and interests.

Ask Place-Questions

Not only will your content be influenced by purpose-questions and by person-questions, it will actually be influenced by questions related to place. You must learn all you can about the basic LOCATION of your speech. You need to know where you are going to present it. I am not just talking about a general location here. I am talking about the fact that you need to know where in the place you will give your presentation. You ask – "Will it be here – or over there? How will the room be arranged? What possible distractions could occur while I am in this place? Where will I put any visual aids that I might choose to use?" Although it may be a stretch here, let me also suggest that you should be very concerned about the "place" on the clock – "What time will I give my speech? How long am I to speak? If I start later than scheduled, am I to go longer than was pre-arranged? Or, do I speak for less than the scheduled length of time?"

Please remember this, the place where you speak may prove to have everything in the world to do with the content that you choose to pour into your speech. For example, if you are asked to speak in a huge, open gymnasium, then you need to prepare for distractions, noise vacuums, and audience-eyes that tend to focus on everybody and everything – except you. If, for example, you have been asked to present to your class, and if you do not know how much moving-room you will have in your particular speaking-location, you may well be up against the wall.

These place-questions are extremely important. Take them seriously.

Ask Process-Questions

Perhaps most importantly, your content will be shaped by process-questions. Process-questions have everything to do with two issues – the development of your subject or topic, and the development of your speech-structure.

Answer the process-questions correctly. Process your content through this filter – "Is my content correct, clear, and credible (believable)?"

You must ask, answer, and master questions related to PROCESS. You can do it – as long as you have also asked and appropriately answered, purpose, person, and place-questions.

Before we close out this section on the content, I want to share much more about the process-questions.

K-I-S-S

For our purposes, K-I-S-S means KEEP IT SIMPLE, SMARTY (not stupid). Remember, The Lynx System emphasizes smart-vision, keen-sightedness – a brightness. Focus on your "smartness" – and concentrate on simplicity.

Your subject and your structure can be determined by three big questions. You will be very smart to ask and answer these simple questions. They will surface later in our book when we address "The

Construction." But for now, as they relate to content, I want to share them with you.

The Three Biggies

The process-questions that you must learn to ask are: "WHAT? – WHY? – HOW?" Get them down. Learn them well. They equal the process – the steps – the procedures that will help you select and structure content. They equal a way for you to "keep it simple, smarty." They are a big reason why speaking with confidence in public can become so easy.

The What?

You ask – "What is the subject? What is the place, event, or philosophy that is the center of this speech?" Now, it might be that you have to use "Who?" – not "What?". Your question might be – "Who is the subject of this speech?" You could even ask – "What, or who, is the core of the entertainment – the center of the 'show' speech?" Let me share examples of some of the "What?" questions and how they shape content.

"What is the "Show" here? Is it life's silly situations? Is it stand-up comedy?"

"What is the "Tell" here? Is it life in Sydney, Australia? Is it America's early space adventures?"

"What is the "Sell" here? Is it the story of polluted water in a particular river? Is it a description of a specific weight-lifting program?"

"Who is the "Tell" or "Sell" here? What is significant about her? What did he offer the world?"

Appropriate "What?" and "Who?" questions help form your content – both subject-wise and structure-wise.

The Why?

You ask questions such as "Why is this relevant? Why did this happen? Why are we not learning from this? Why did she do that? Why is this funny? Why is it interesting? Why does it call for an immediate response?"

The appropriate "Why?" questions help form the subject and structure the content.

The How?

You ask "How?" questions that help solidify the subject and structure of your content. You ask – "How can the funny – or the entertaining – serve the audience? What will they enjoy? How can they apply what they learn about the importance of athletics as it relates to team building skills? How can they respond to the 'What?' and the 'Why?' that I have presented to them? How can they feel about this? How can they act about this?"

Be A Good "Questioneer"

Remember, your content is birthed by the very questions you ask. Ask, and appropriately answer purpose-questions. Ask, and appropriately answer person-questions. Ask, and appropriately answer place-questions. Ask, and appropriately answer process-questions ("What? – Why? – How?").

Keep Them Specific

When I was in high school, I was a weekend broadcaster. I had a tremendous amount of fun working at the radio station. At this point, I want to tell you, that when it comes to speaking with confidence in public, the fun is not in broadcasting – the fun is in "narrowcasting." BE A NARROWCASTER. Ask specific questions. Build topics that are specific in nature. Narrowcast – do not broadcast.

For example, do not speak on "Challenges Teenagers Face," speak on "Learning How To Speak With Confidence Is As Simple As C, C, C, And C." Do not speak on "Rules Are Always Bad," speak on "The 10 O'Clock Curfew For High School Students Should Be Questioned." Do not speak on "Democracy," speak on "Teenagers In America Have Significant Educational Opportunities Because . . ." Do not speak on "This Is My Life," speak on "The Most Memorable Moment In My Life."

If you want a strong response from your audience, then present them with a narrow focus. When it comes to speaking with confidence in public, NARROW IS IN.

This Is It

At this point, it will be helpful to share an example that briefly capsules a narrow topic and the "What? – Why? – How?" technique for birthing content.

The Topic: Our Town River Is Sick.

The What?: You paint a word-picture of a bad situation – a polluted river.

The Why?: You diagnose, or analyze, why it is sick – greed, ignorance, apathy.

The How?: You share how we should feel (concerned, angry, determined). You also share how we can act (examples – letters to Congress, product boycotts, lead our community in a recycling program).

What I want you to remember about The CONTENT of your 4C challenge is this – you play the key role. You must be the "questioneer" – you must be a good "questioneer" – you must answer the questions you ask appropriately. And, remember – keep it simple smarty!

The Content

Chapter Summary

- Build solid Content.
  Be a good "questioneer."
- Ask PURPOSE-QUESTIONS –
  "Is it Show, Tell, or Sell?"
- Ask PERSON-QUESTIONS –
  "Who is my audience?"
- Ask PLACE-QUESTIONS –
  "Where will I deliver my speech?"
- Ask PROCESS-QUESTIONS –
  "What? – Why? – How?"
- Be a "narrowcaster."

CHAPTER 10

The Construction
You Are An "Engineer"

You have asked and appropriately answered your purpose-questions, your person-questions, your place-questions, and your process-questions (What? – Why? – How?) questions. You have been a good "questioneer." Now, you shift from content-emphasis to construction-emphasis. You shift from your role as a "questioneer" to your role as an "engineer." Now, you are ready to CONSTRUCT your "speech-house."

There are many floor plans from which you could choose as you seek to build your speech-house plan. Possible speech-house plans could be built upon the following: alphabetical listings, numerical listings, and chronological listings. However, since this is not an exhaustive analysis of every possible plan, I think it best if I lay out for you the one plan I most often suggest. This plan is basically the "Sell" speech.

The Five Room Speech-Plan

As you construct your speech-house from the content your "questioneering" has provided, you will want to consider using THE FIVE ROOM SPEECH-PLAN. When you utilize The Five Room Plan, you allow your content to fall into one of five rooms.

Let me now give a name to each of the five rooms:
1) the INTRODUCTION
2) the "WHAT?"
3) the "WHY?"
4) the "HOW?"
5) the CONCLUSION.

A Resurfacing

You will notice the resurfacing, or reappearance, of the concept that equals our "What? – Why? – How?" This is not by accident; it is by intent. There is an intentional correlation, or relatedness, between the appearance of the "What? – Why? – How?" in the content phase of our discussion, and the reappearance of the "What? – Why? – How?" in the construction phase of our time together.

Now, as we ponder your role as an "engineer" in the construction phase, we discover that the "What? – Why? – How?" actually become the three center-rooms of our house plan – or the three phases of the body of the speech.

Again, it is important to note that the introduction comes before this speech-body, the conclusion comes after this speech-body.

The Introduction Room

The Lynx Speak-In-Public Learning System For High School Students says this – "Never start a speech. Always introduce a speech."

THE MISSING LYNX

Remember this – there is a tremendous difference between starting your speech and introducing your speech. If you simply start your speech, you choose to construct a four room house. A four room house will not work here. You must have five rooms!

Listening can be a chore for your audience. You want to do everything you can do to make listening to you an easy choice for your audience – not a chore. Certainly, you understand high school students. You understand how busy your minds can be. If you simply start your speech, you will never fully grab the attention of your audience.

INTRODUCE YOUR SPEECH. You will have a much better chance to catch the attention of your audience. An introduction need not be long – but it must be strong.

The 3E Test

Your introduction must pass the 3E test. It must:

1) earn the attention of the audience
2) express your topic
3) excite your audience about what is to come.

Earn Their Attention

Catch your audience by surprise! Discover what most everyone else might do, and try a different approach. Let your style show through. Your teacher can assist you.

Create suspense! Indicate that something exciting is about to happen. You want everyone to "listen up" and pay attention.

Communicate through story! Everyone loves a good story. A good story can earn their attention. The "catching," the "creating," and the "communicating" help EARN the attention of your audience.

Express Your Topic

Your introduction is the room, or the place, where you make very clear the topic you are addressing. As I said earlier, you can create an atmosphere of suspense, or even curiosity, as to the specifics that are to follow – but there should be no second guessing about the basic topic you are presenting. In your introduction, you EXPRESS your topic.

You might want to ponder the following idea-starters:

"Today, our topic equals a huge question . . ."

"Within the next fifteen minutes, I will examine the pros and cons of . . ."

"Something mighty important happened last month in Congress. I hope it never happens again. Here's the story . . ."

"It has to stop – before I go any further, let me repeat – it has to stop. Now, let me introduce what I call the 'challenge of the century' . . ."

A Good Title Can Help You

If you are familiar with my core-thinking, you know that I strongly believe that any strength can be taken too far – so far that it becomes problematical. For example, eye contact can be taken so far that it begins to equal a "staring down" of another. Accordingly, before I share specifically how a title might help you express your topic in your introduction, let me caution you that this very concept can be taken too far. Please do not overuse it.

With that said, let me state that I have found that an expression and enhancement of the very title of my presentation can sometimes work as an effective introduction. Let me share a couple of examples with you.

One of my speeches is titled – "Like A Pelican In The Desert." When I introduce this presentation, I might simply state, as the very first words out of my mouth, the following:

Like A Pelican In The Desert . . . Pelican – large water bird with an ostensible pouch designed for the scooping up of fish. Desert – dry, barren spanse of land. Have you ever felt "like a pelican in the desert?" Have you ever been asked to lead a project without any leadership experience whatsoever? Have you ever been asked to do something that you have never done before? Of course you have. The purpose of this speech is to: 1) spend a little time defining that sensation of awkwardness – particularly when new leadership opportunities face you, 2) spend a little time analyzing why you feel awkward about the situation, and 3) spend a great deal of time sharing with you how you can respond here – what you can do to remedy the situation – so you can move beyond the awkward feeling – beyond feeling "like a pelican in the desert."

Another one of my speech-titles is "Think Like A Giraffe." When I introduce the speech, I might choose to say the following words:

Think Like A Giraffe – I bet you have never thought about "thinking like a giraffe." I invite you to do so now. I encourage you to "stick your neck out" now. We are gathered here to address the issue of speaking in public. And, if you and I are to do our best, then we must "think like a giraffe." Too many speakers are boring. The content of their speech, and the delivery of their speech, is dull. (Notice I just did a WHAT?.) Normally, their content and their delivery is weak because they have not paid the preparation price. They did not work. They did not practice. (Notice I just shared a WHY?.) But, you can do better – you can "think like a giraffe." (Notice that I am beginning to share a HOW?.) You can learn how to be much more creative, much more effective, much more exciting. In our time together this afternoon, you can learn how to "think like a giraffe." You can learn to work on three specific things – the direction of your thinking – the discipline of your approach – the delight you bring to journey. Now, let us get started. Let us "think like a giraffe" – and reach for the sky.

Remember, one of the purposes of the introduction is to express your topic.

Excite Your Audience About What Is To Come

In your introduction, you must not only earn the attention of the audience, you must not only express your topic, you must also EXCITE your audience about what is to come. Although I tried to do that in the previous "Think Like A Giraffe" example, let me state more about what it means to "excite an audience" with an introduction.

Remember, you are competing for your audience's attention. The fundamental burden for their listening is upon your shoulders. It is your responsibility to build enthusiasm. The introduction is the perfect place to start doing that. In the introduction, you can crescendo with your voice. In the introduction, you can stun them with statistics. In the introduction, you can whet their appetite – encourage them to want more.

You can encourage your audience to "stay tuned." An effective introduction makes it easier for an audience member to say, "Yes, I want more. She is taking this seriously. She has paid the preparation-price. This is something I choose to listen to. I'm actually excited about hearing more."

When you excite your audience about what is to come in the remaining four rooms of your speech-house, you are creating something. You are creating expectancy. An introduction should do precisely that – CREATE EXPECTANCY.

The "What?" Room

The second room in the speech-house that you construct, or engineer, is The "What?" Room. It is the front layer of the body of your speech. If your purpose is to "put on a show," what I refer to as the "Show" speech, your "What?" sets the stage for you.

If your purpose is to inform, what I refer to as the "Tell" speech, you refer to a person, place, event, or an activity. Your "What?" simply contains a description of the person, place, event, or activity.

If your purpose is to elicit a more active response from your audience, to persuade your audience – to give a "Sell" speech – if you want to affect the attitude and behavior of your audience, then your "What?" equals a description of a specific challenge or opportunity.

For much of our time together, the "Sell" speech–purpose will equal a major opportunity.

For now, please remember this – your "What?" room may look like DESCRIPTION or DEFINITION.

Your "What?" room, the first room in the body of your speech, paints a picture of a specific problem or a particular opportunity that you have just introduced. Here, you lay out what the problem or opportunity looks like, what is happening, what is not happening, whom it is harming, or whom it may one day help.

This May Help

Speaking of helping, this may help you understand the "What?" room. Imagine you are sick. You go to your doctor. Your doctor asks you to describe for him how you feel. You attempt to paint a word-picture of your problem for the doctor. Before the doctor can DIAGNOSE (the "Why?") and PRESCRIBE (the "How?"), you must DESCRIBE (the "What?").

In a similar fashion, you can use your "What?" room to paint a picture of a particular challenge: the polluted Town River, the starving inner city, a diminished Rainforest.

The "Why?" Room

Your next step is to analyze the "What?" room. You DISSECT it. You DIAGNOSE it. You ask "Why?" questions about the "What?" room – "Why is this important? Why is it happening? Why is it worth attention – attitudes – actions?"

Quite simply, your "Why?" room helps you build your case, helps you justify your position – prepares your audience for the "How?" that is to follow.

The "How?" Room

In most instances, the "How?" room is where you will choose to spend a significant portion of your speech-time.

If you are simply telling us about someone, some place, an event, or an activity, you suggest how we can enjoy it or how we can learn from it. Even if your speech is a "Show" speech, if you are seeking to entertain us, you may choose to share with us how laughter or humor can help us.

However, if you are trying to do more than "Show" or even "Tell," if you are wanting to "Sell" us an attitude and an action, then it is mandatory that you present us with a "How?." Your "Sell" speech has to have a "How?."

This is terribly important. Do not simply describe for us a bad situation. Do not simply explain to us why it is bad. Give us some hope. Give us some remedies. Give us some ideas. Inspire within us some ATTITUDES. Inspire us toward ACTION! For example, you may encourage us to value our health (attitude). To this end, you may also advise us not to eat the food in the school cafeteria (behavior). Just teasing!

The "Conclusion" Room

Finally, in room number five, the heart-room, you bring it all together.

Just as you do not start a speech, you introduce a speech – you do not stop a speech, you conclude a speech.

The 4S Test

Your conclusion must pass the 4S test. It must:
1) signal closure
2) switch back to the introduction
3) summarize your central theme
4) send an invitation.

Signal Closure

Your conclusion must SIGNAL that the end of your speech is close at hand. It suggests that you will soon stop speaking.

"Suggested closure" is important here because it influences your audiences' expectations. It is my experience that audiences instinctively seem to listen to a concluding portion of a presentation – if they clearly understand that the final statements of your speech are on their way.

The following language-choices may assist you in indicating closure: "In conclusion" . . . "To summarize" . . . "Let me review" . . . "We have examined our 'What?,' 'Why?,' and 'How?' – now, let us bring it all together."

Switch Back To The Introduction

A SWITCHING-BACK to the introduction of your speech is an appropriate indication that the conclusion of your speech is indeed underway. But that is not the only reason that your conclusion should switch back to your introduction. Your switching-back will emphasize the central theme of your presentation. It glues the ending portion of your presentation to the body-portion and to the introduction-portion of your speech.

You can directly state, as you are concluding your speech, that, just for a moment, you want to refer back to your introduction. However, I prefer a passive, or indirect, switching-back.

For example, one of my presentations is titled "The Art Of Killing Kudzu – Management By

Encouragement." In the introduction of my presentation, I establish the fact that the vine known as kudzu can grow wild and choke out "good stuff" – corn, beans, cucumbers. In the body of the presentation of this particular speech, I build a case for comparing an out-of-control, negative attitude in the workplace to kudzu in a garden. I further indicate that there is something that can kill this type of business-like kudzu. I call the business-kudzu killing chemical "encouragement." Now, in the introduction of the speech, I have made it very clear that kudzu is "bad stuff." In the conclusion of the speech, I simply restate that kudzu is "bad stuff." However, in the conclusion I continue by saying the following: "Yes, kudzu is bad stuff. However, management by encouragement is good stuff. Management by encouragement can kill kudzu."

I encourage you to be sure your conclusions switch back to your introductions.

Summarize The Central Theme

Not only should your conclusion signal closure and switch back to the introduction, it should also SUMMARIZE the central thrust of your speech.

Your conclusion should make it easy for us to carry home with us the key points of your presentation.

Send An Invitation

Finally, your conclusion should SEND an invitation. This has been a central theme of our time together, but I want to state it afresh here. In your conclusion, you send an invitation for your audience to feel a certain way and to do a certain thing. You want them to R.S.V.P. You say to them, "Please respond." You invite them to FEEL a certain way and to DO a certain thing. For example:

> "Care about our community (attitude) –
> join the Key Club (behavior)."

> "Care about our baseball team (attitude) –
> come to this afternoon's game (behavior)."

> "Care about Town River (attitude) –
> come this Saturday morning to clean the
> banks around the bridge (behavior)."

Yes, your conclusion must pass the 4S test: it must signal closure, it must switch-back, it must summarize your central thrust, it must send an invitation. And when your conclusion has done that, you have completed your five room speech-house. And it is something to behold! It is something to hear!! It is something to experience!!!

Put Furniture In Your Rooms

It is not enough to build a solid, five room speech-house. You will want to add furniture to your rooms.

If the five rooms form the outline of your speech, then the furniture equals what I call the "extra stuff." If your outline equals the skeleton of your speech, then the furniture, or the "extra stuff," equals the "meat on the skeleton – the meat on the outline."

I have tried to illustrate this "meat on the outline" concept throughout this book. I am illustrating this very concept when I compare the outline of a speech to the five room plan, and when I compare the "meat on the skeleton" to the furniture you should place in your rooms.

In your house, your furniture can equal bookcases, tables, chairs, bedroom suites, living room suites, dining room suites, or sofa-beds. In your speech-house rooms, your furniture can equal statistics, or examples, or definitions, or stories, or illustrations.

Just as you do not want to fill your home with nothing but beds, you will want to bless your speech-house with different types of furniture. This book is literally full of a variety of speech-furniture pieces. Study them. Learn from them.

As you work on your speech-house, you can rearrange your furniture. There might be a time when you decide to move an illustration that you orginally had placed in your "What?" room to the Conclusion room for the sake of emphasis.

As you begin to "get a feel" for how your speech impacts your audiences, you may choose to begin with your strongest illustration – rather than saving it for last.

Build a solid five room speech-house. Then, place into it a mixture of furniture that functions.

Chapter Summary

- Build a strong speech-house. Be a good "engineer."
- Use the Five Room Speech-Plan.
- The Five Rooms equal the INTRODUC-TION, the "WHAT?", the "WHY?," the "HOW?," and the CONCLUSION.
- The Introduction must pass the 3E test: earn – express – excite.
- The "What?" describes.
- The "Why?" dissects.
- The "How?" prescribes – "how to feel" (attitude) – "what to do" (behavior).
- The Conclusion must pass the 4S Test: signal – switch – summarize – send.
- Place furniture in your speech-house – the "meat on the outline" – statistics, examples, definitions, stories, or illustrations.
- It is okay to rearrange your speech-house furniture.

CHAPTER 11

The Carrying

You Are A "Transporter"

O nce you marry your CONTENT to your CONSTRUCTION, once you intertwine your role as "questioneer" with your role as "engineer," you are ready for The CARRYING. As a "transporter," you are responsible for transporting – or carrying – or delivering your speech from yourself to your audience.

You have the responsibility of driving your speech to your audience.

How do you do that? How do you carry – or deliver – or transport your speech?

Well, the first thing you notice is that I did not place one particular verb alongside the before-mentioned verbs. I used – "deliver" – "carry" – and "transport." I intentionally omitted the verb "haul."

You Do Not Haul Speeches

Mules haul loads. You and I carry or deliver speeches. Mules normally operate under a heavy burden. As speakers, you and I do not need to operate under a heavy burden.

As I observed my students speak before me, they often acted as if they felt like they were "hauling" a speech. They were acting like their speech was very heavy.

Lynx-like speeches are not heavy. Remember, they are light. You do not have to haul them. You can carry – or transport – or deliver them.

Carrying Wheels Will Help

There are four CARRYING WHEELS that will help you transport your speech-house to your audience. These four carrying-wheels help make speaking with confidence in public much easier than you might have imagined.

The four carrying wheels that I invite you to consider at this point are:

1) your eyes
2) your voice
3) your body
4) visual aids.

Your Eyes Can Help You

Do not underestimate the power of your eyes. Do not resort to silly techniques that seek to give people the impression you are looking at them – when in reality you are not looking at them.

Your goal is this – you want each member of your audience to feel like you have looked at him or her on several occasions during your presentation. Now, for this to occur, you must be familiar with your presentation. You must be so familiar with your presentation that your eyes are not tied to your speech.

For our purposes, in *The Missing Lynx*, there are four methods of delivery. The manner in which you use your eyes has everything in the world to do with the delivery-system you use. You can read your speech. I refer to this as the manuscript-delivery. I do not encourage you to read your entire speech. You can memorize your speech. I do not encourage you to do that. Your speech will seem phony, insincere, contrived.

You can deliver your speech with the assistance of notes, or lists. I encourage you to choose this system. Your eyes can work for you through the list-system of delivery. Incidentally, a fourth system of delivery is the learned method. Here, you simply have learned your speech. There is a huge difference between learning your speech (this is natural in its delivery) and memorizing a speech (this is not natural in its delivery).

The amazing thing is this. As you use the list-system of delivery, as you become more and more familiar with your speech and The Lynx Speak-In-Public Learning System, confidence begins to find you. You may actually move from delivering list-aided speeches to delivering learned presentations.

My point is this. In the list-aided system of delivery, and in the learned type of delivery, YOUR EYES CAN WORK FOR YOU.

And that is what you want them to do. You want your eyes to help you deliver your presentation. You want your eyes to carry your speech from within you to your audience. You do not want your notes to control you. You want to control your notes so your eyes can work for you.

Now, before I close out this section, I want to be very honest with you. Your first few presentations may indeed be presentations that you have to read. My hope is this – as you speak more and more, you will find yourself able to read less and less. And as you read LESS AND LESS, your eyes can work for you MORE AND MORE!

Remember, this whole concept of growth as it relates to speaking in public is process – not event. I well understand that sometimes we have to take small steps before we can take large steps.

Your Voice Can Help You

Yes, your eyes help you carry your message. Your voice can also deliver the key points of your message. Please understand, your voice can effectively transport – carry – your message from you to your audience – when you learn to VARY YOUR VOICE.

"Vary" is an important verb. Basically, it means to alter – or to change. Your voice will help you carry – or deliver – your presentation when you vary:

    1) the VOLUME of the sound

    2) the SPEED with which you speak

    3) the INFLECTION of your voice – the range, or city, in which your voice chooses to live.

Your Body Can Help You

Not only can your words help you, not only can your eyes and voice help you, your whole body can assist you in carrying your speech from yourself to your audience.

Worded another way, if it is not overdone, if it is not predictable, and if it is not distractive, the movement of your body can help you carry – or transport – or deliver – your speech from yourself to your audience. Accordingly, vary the position of your body. Let your hands and head move freely. Let your face smile – or frown – when it seems natural. LET YOUR BODY TALK.

Again, be careful here. Do not allow the movement of your body to become overdone – or "predictable" – or distractive. This is a struggle for me. For the most part, movement enhances my presentations. But, on occasion, without doubt, I have taken "movement" too far – so far that it became distractive for some members of the audience. I remind you and myself here – BALANCE, or appropriateness, is the key.

Vary the movement of your body. Catch your audience by surprise. Use the "carrying wheels" that equal the movement of your body carefully.

Visual Aids Can Help You

I almost omitted this brief section on "visual aids" – charts, graphs, handouts, objects, and exhibits. I have obviously chosen to address it – but only briefly.

Do not use visual aids as an "easy way out" – as a "cop out." This does not serve anyone well. The Lynx System is easy – but it is not the "easy way out" – it is not a "cop out."

Do not let visual aids hinder you or your audience. Visual aids might, on occasion, help you – if you use them carefully. USE VISUAL AIDS SPARINGLY.

Remember the following about visual aids:
- Visual Aids need to be crisp, clean, clear – very easy to read.
- As a high school student, you should limit the use of visual aids to very small audiences.
- In most instances, visual aids should not become the center of your speech. Visual aids rarely make the "three-pointer." They normally get the credit for the "assist." (What did I just do? I used an instance from basketball – "the one who scores the three-pointer" as opposed to "the one who assists" to illustrate the support role of the visual aid. Let me add that this concept of illustration is covered in *Celebrate The Butterflies*, pages 75-89. The section dealing with "just as" material beginning on page 79 should prove especially beneficial.)
- For our purposes, your visual aids should be short, simple, and specific.
- Visual aids should not come between you and your audience. Try not to turn your back on your audience when referring to your visual aids.

Visual aids will work adequately as "carrying wheels." However, at this stage in your speaking-experience, you should not significantly rely on visual aids. Unless instructed to do so by your teacher, or unless circumstances require as much, concentrate on what you can do with your words – your eyes – your voice – your body. Develop these expression-skills. The legitimate opportunity to use visual aids will come soon enough. For now, focus on what you can do with the "carrying wheels" that equal your eyes, your voice, and your body.

A Restatement

Because these "carrying wheels" are crucial to the effectiveness of your speech, I want to address them one more time – to restate – perhaps using different words – the necessity of utilizing "carrying wheels."

Remember, it is not enough to write a great speech. It is not enough to have good speech-content -- and good speech-construction – you must deliver, or carry, or transport your speech. It is not enough to be a fine "Questioneer," and a super "Engineer" – you must also be an effective "Transporter" – a carrier – not a "hauler." The speech must not become a burden that you haul. It is not that heavy. It is light – as long as you follow The Lynx Speak-In-Public Learning System For High School Students.

Again, you will need four carrying wheels:

1) Your EYES show your sincerity, your preparation, your emphasis, your "connection."

2) Your VOICE can make the difference between "lazy" speech and "lively" speech. Vary your voice.

3) Your BODY can talk. Try not to use podiums. Be natural. Remember, there is power in "presence" – there is power in your "best posture" – there can certainly be power in appropriate movement. Let your arms "wiggle" when you feel it to be a natural extension of the point you are seeking to make.

4) Your VISUAL AIDS, when appropriate, can be helpful – if you keep them crisp and clear – short and simple.

The Carrying

Chapter Summary

- As a "carrier" you transport speeches from yourself to your audience.
- Do not haul speeches – "carry them."
- Use "carrying wheels" – your eyes, your voice, your movement, and your visual aids.

CHAPTER 12

The Connection

You Are An "Impacter"

his is another one of those "I cannot wait to get to it" sections. My friends, there is a wonderful connection-feeling that occurs when you craft and carry, design and deliver, tailor and transport your presentation. (Now what did I just do? I used alliterative pairings – words that begin with identical letters – to describe the writing and the presenting of the speech. This can be very helpful to you and your audience. It can provide both structure and sequence. Take alliterative pairing seriously.)

For now, let us move back to the basic point here. When you do both well – write well and present well – you have a great chance to "make a connection" with your audience. This is good. This is great.

Making The CONNECTION through your speech is similar to:

- hitting a tee shot 250 yards – in the right direction
- hooking and landing a 24 inch native trout – using a fly rod
- presenting a ninety minute piano concert, note free – and receiving a tremendous standing ovation
- hitting a grand slam home run – in the final game of the state championship tournament
- throwing a baton fifty feet high – and catching it with authority
- pinning your opponent in the state championship wrestling match – thirty seconds into the match
- doing your best at what you love to do – even if it does not mean coming in first place.

The Connection

It is the feel. It is the connection. It is TOUCHSPEECH – something special that happens between you and your audience. (Touchspeech is discussed in *Celebrate The Butterflies*, pages 147-151.) When you "make the connection," you bring things full-circle. You have thrown – they have caught. You have given – they have received. You have challenged – they have responded. And, your whole being shouts, "Yes!"

The other Cs – The Content, The Construction, The Carrying, have now culminated in The Connection. You were a "questioneer." You were an "engineer." You were a "transporter." Now, you are an "impacter." And, it is making a difference for your audience.

It will not always happen. It certainly does not always happen with me. Even when I do my best, some just do not get it. And, they may not be able to help it. I like to tell myself that their "inside stuff" – a headache, or a cold, or a test they know they have failed, and their "outside stuff" – the noise, the heat, or a glance toward the window might be distracting them. I may be able to do little about it.

However, when I do experience The Connection – a good feeling – The Touchspeech, it helps me give more – it helps me grow more.

I believe the same can be true for you.

Through the speeches you write and present, you can make a huge difference. You can make a positive IMPACT on the lives of your audience, and yourself.

Chapter Summary

- Make The CONNECTION.
- Impact your audience.
- Appreciate the feeling.
- Create Touchspeech.

Part Four

The Lynx List

CHAPTER 13

The Top 20 List

Reminders, Not Replacements

Certainly there will be moments when you will appreciate a Ready-Reference – a quick glance into The Lynx Speak-In-Public Learning System For High School Students. Accordingly, I present here a reminder-list that very briefly lays out for you some of the key words and concepts that merge to form The Lynx System.

Please remember this – these are only trigger-words. They certainly do not capsule any specific segment in *The Missing Lynx*.

These words can quickly remind you of what you have read. That is the key here – REMINDERS – not replacements. Our Top 20 List equals trigger-thoughts – nothing more.

The Top 20 Reference List

1) Build solid Content.
   Be a good "questioneer."

2) Ask PURPOSE-QUESTIONS –
   "Is it Show, Tell, or Sell?"

3) Ask PERSON-QUESTIONS –
   "Who is my audience?"

4) Ask PLACE-QUESTIONS –
   "Where?"

5) Ask PROCESS-QUESTIONS –
   "What? – Why? – How?"

6) Construct a strong speech-house.
   Be a good "engineer."

7) Use the Five Room Speech-Plan.

8) The Five Rooms equal:
   the INTRODUCTION
   the "WHAT?"
   the "WHY?"
   the "HOW?" and
   the CONCLUSION.

9) The Introduction must pass the 3E test:
   earn – express – excite.

10) The "What?" describes.

11) The "Why?" dissects.

12) The "How?" prescribes – "how to feel"
    (attitude) – "what to do" (behavior).

13) The Conclusion must pass the 4S Test:
    signal – switch – summarize – send.

14) Place furniture in your speech-house –
    the "meat on the outline" – statistics,
    examples, definitions, or illustrations.

15) As a "carrier," you transport speeches from yourself to your audience.

16) Do not haul speeches – "carry them."

17) Use "carrying wheels" –
your eyes, your voice, your movement, and your visual aids.

18) Make The CONNECTION.

19) Impact your audience.

20) Appreciate the feeling –
The Touchspeech.

(The above model is for the "Sell" speech. It can be modified for the "Tell" and "Show" speeches.)

Part Five
The Lasting
Lynx

CHAPTER 14

Let It Last

L et two thoughts last for a lifetime.
Speaking in public is lynx-like. It is
light, not heavy. You have every
capacity to be lynx-eyed – keen-
sighted, bright! Yes, YOU CAN DO THIS. And, the
skills you are learning will LAST FOR A LIFETIME!

In tennis, when a particular player (example,
"Player Jones") wins the first point after deuce (even
score), that player is considered the one with an advantage. The umpire announces the name of the player
with the advantage (example, "Advantage Jones").

In school, in business, in the whole of life, you will be placed in "deuce" situations – or "even" situations – or very competitive situations. On the surface, you and others will appear to be evenly matched. However, if you possess the ability to speak and communicate with confidence, you will have a huge advantage. When all else is the same – when it is "deuce" – your ability to present with confidence can give you the "BIG WIN." Why? Because it will have simply been "Advantage Speaker." The skills you now learn last a lifetime and gift you with a PERPETUAL ADVANTAGE.

Chapter Summary

- This can last.
- You can be "Advantage Speaker."

CHAPTER 15

Take Me Seriously

I have honestly tried to help you through this book. Through intent, I have not attempted to cover all that which equals the challenge of speaking and communicating with confidence in public. I have attempted to anticipate some of your major questions and concerns.

It has been my desire to share concepts – and then, on occasion, illustrate these concepts with examples that might prove helpful. The results, of course, are up to you. I do know I have tried to help. But, I do want to make one more "try" – one more swing – one more cast.

THE MISSING LYNX

I believe strongly in what I said at the beginning of this book. The skill of speaking and communicating with confidence in public is becoming increasingly important. And, for the most part, we have increasingly ignored it at the high school level. For certain, some wonderful teachers and parents have been positive reinforcers and remarkable tutors in this area. But, in the mainstream, we have let you down. In this book, I tried to do something about the situation.

You will certainly have questions. In that case, I encourage you to speak with your teacher, to secure a copy of my book *Celebrate The Butterflies – Speaking With Confidence In Public*, or to refer to the other books listed in my recommended reading list.

Should you still have questions, I encourage you to write or e-mail me – or even call me. I will do my best to respond to your question. (See page 149.)

I may not be able to respond immediately – but I should be able to respond within a week or two. So do not wait until the last minute. Naturally, the fundamental structure of your speech is not something that I can address. That would not be appropriate. But I will be more than willing to respond to a couple of specific questions. Please take me seriously here.

In fact, I hope you do what someone did with me just this morning. I was heading back to Atlanta after a presentation in another city. As is my custom, I purchased a couple of cookies in the airport, and planned to enjoy them during the flight. I was hungry.

About five minutes after boarding the plane, I began writing the concluding portions of this very book. My cookies were placed in my lap, adjacent to my notebook.

A delightful lady walked by me, headed toward her seat behind me, and noticed my cookies. She said, "Lucky you. Cookies." Instinctively, I responded, "Do you want one?" She said, "Yes, I will be back." To my surprise, she came back. I shared.

Surprise me. I would love to share with you. Keep me posted on your progress.

Speak well,
Stephen M. Gower, CSP
Fall 1998

Recommended Reading

Booher, Dianna. *Communicate With Confidence! How To Say It Right The First Time, And Every Time.* New York: Mc Graw-Hill, 1994.

Brooks, William T. *High Impact Public Speaking.* New Jersey: Prentice Hall, 1988.

Cook, Jeff Scott. *The Elements Of Speech Writing And Public Speaking.* New York: Macmillan, 1991.

Decker, Bert. *You've Got To Be Believed To Be Heard.* New York: St. Martin's Press, 1992.

Durham, Ken. *Speaking From The Heart.* Fort Worth: Sweet Publishing, 1986.

Gower, Stephen M. *Celebrate The Butterflies – Presenting With Confidence In Public.* Toccoa: Lectern Publishing, 1993.

Jeffery, Robert C. and Owen Patterson. *Speech: A Basic Text.* New York: Harper & Row, 1989.

Maggio, Rosalie. *How To Say It: Choice Words, Phrases, Sentences, And Paragraphs For Every Situation.* New Jersey: Prentice Hall, 1990.

Makay, John J. *Public Speaking: Theory Into Practice.* Fort Worth: Harcourt Brace Jovanovich College Publishers, 1992.

Mouat, Lawrence Henry. *A Guide To Effective Public Speaking.* Boston: D.C. Heath and Company, 1959.

Peoples, David. *Presentations Plus.* New York: John Wiley & Sons, 1988.

Rozakis, Laurie E. *The Complete Idiot's Guide To Speaking In Public With Confidence.* New York: Alpha Books, 1995.

Schloff, Laurie and Maricia Yudkin. *Smart Speaking.* New York: Penguin, 1992.

Slutsky, Jeff and Michael Aun. *The Toastmasters International Guide To Successful Speaking.* Chicago: Dearborn Financial Publishing, 1997.

Recommended Reading

Stuart, Christina. *How To Be An Effective Public Speaker.* Chicago: NTC Publishing, 1989.

Stuttard, Marie. *The Power Of Speech.* New York: Barron's, 1994.

Van Ekeren, Glenn. *The Speaker's Sourcebook: Quotes, Stories, And Anecdotes For Every Occasion.* New Jersey: Prentice Hall, 1988.

Walton, Donald. *Are You Communicating? You Can't Manage Without It.* New York: Mc Graw-Hill, 1989.

Reference Resources

For our purposes, this Reference Resources section stands apart from the Recommended Reading category. I thought it would be helpful to you if I listed a grouping of books that would give you ideas for that which I refer to as speech-house furniture. In other words, I am sharing information that you will want to consider for anecdotes, quotations, stories, statistics, definitions and descriptions.

This information is not aimed toward specific topics as much as it is pointed toward possible examples. On occasion, topical ideas may be suggested – but that is certainly not the thrust of this listing. You must choose your own topic. I have intentionally omitted more topics than I have included. I am not seeking to provide you with topics as much as I am examples. This is an important differentiation. For the most part, what you discover in these next pages will be idea-extenders. You provide the basic idea.

Be careful how you use this material. Use it sparingly, use it appropriately – do not use it offensively. In no way do I intend to endorse the use of any inappropriate illustrations. My intent here is simply to provide you with a large catalogue of options.

Remember, your pieces of furniture – your "meat on the outline" – can help you enhance, explain, and expand your outline-points. It is as if the content from these books can, when appropriate, serve as a hinge that opens the door of understanding for your audience.

Biographies/Viewpoints

General

Churchill, Winston. *My Early Life.* New York: Charles Scribner and Sons, 1958.

Degregoria, William. *The Complete Book Of U.S. Presidents*. New York: Barricade, 1993.

Dyer, Wayne. *Wisdom Of The Ages*. New York: Harper Collins, 1998.

Ellis, Joseph. *American Sphinx – The Character Of Thomas Jefferson*. New York: Vintage, 1998.

Lindbergh, Charles. *The Spirit Of St. Louis*. St. Paul: Minnesota Historical Society, 1953.

Lowe, Janet. *Warren Buffett Speaks*. New York: John Wiley and Sons, 1997.

Lowe, Janet. *Jack Welsh Speaks*. New York: John Wiley and Sons, 1998.

African Americans

Delany, Sarah and Elizabeth Delany. *Having Our Say*. New York: Kodansha, 1993.

King, Martin Luther. *I Have A Dream – Writings And Speeches That Changed The World*. New York: Harper Collins, 1992.

Lewis, John. *Walking With The Wind – A Memoir Of The Movement*. New York: Simon & Shuster, 1998.

Mullane, Deidre. *Words To Make My Dream Children Live*. New York: Anchor, 1995.

Valde, Roger. *The Essential Black Literature Guide*. Detroit: Visible International, 1996.

White, Deborah. *Too Heavy A Load*. New York: W.W. Norton, 1998.

Latin Americans

Collier, Simon (ed.) *The Cambridge Encylopedia Of Latin America And The Carribean*. New York: Cambridge Press, 1992.

Novas, Himilce. *Everything You Need To Know About Latino History*. New York: Plume, 1998.

Native Americans

Brown, Dee. *Bury My Heart At Wounded Knee - An Indian History Of American West*. New York: Owl, 1970.

Maxwell, James A. (ed.) *America's Facinating Indian Heritage - The First Americans*. Pleasantville NY: Plume, 1997.

Sports

Berra, Yogi. *The Yogi Book*. New York: Workman, 1998.

Reference Resources

Gutman, Bill. *Sammy Sosa.* New York: Archway, 1998.

Hall, Jonathan. *Mark Mc Gwire.* Archway, 1998.

Strug, Kerri. *Landing On My Feet.* Kansas City: Andrews Mc Meel, 1998.

Zimmerman, Jean and Gil Reavill. *Raising Our Athletic Daughters.* New York: Doubleday, 1998.

Women

Asler, Bill. *The Uncommon Wisdom Of Oprah Winfrey.* New York: Carol Publishing, 1997.

Blackman, Ann. *Seasons Of Her Life - The Biography Of Madeline Korbel Albright.* New York: Schribner, 1998.

Glennon, Lorraine (ed). *Ladies Home Journal's 100 Most Influential Women Of The Twentieth Century.* Des Moines: Meridith Corporation, 1998.

Graham, Katherine. *The Oxford Companion To Women's Writing In The United States*. New York: Oxford, 1995.

Morton, Andrew. *Diana – Her True Story*. New York: Pocket Press, 1997.

Thebaud, Francoise. *A History Of Women*. Boston: Harvard Press, 1994.

Quotations

Bartlett, John. *Bartlett's Famous Quotations*. Boston: Little Brown And Company, 1992.

Cohen, M.J. *The Penguin Thesarus Of Quotations*. New York: Penguin Putnam, 1998.

Fitzhenry, Robert. *The Harper Book Of Quotations*. New York: Harper Collins, 1993.

Griessman, Gene. *Words Lincoln Lived By*. New York: Fireside, 1997.

Reference Resources

Kennedy, Max. *Make Gentle The Life Of This World.* New York: Harcourt Brace, 1998.

Miner, Margaret and Hugh Rauson. *Dictionary Of American Quotations.* New York: Penguin Books, 1997.

Spinrad, Leonard and Thelma Spinrad. *Speaker's Lifetime Library.* New Jersey: Prentice Hall, 1997.

Science And Technology

Berkman, Robert. *Find It Fast – How To Uncover Expert Information On Any Subject In Print Or On-Line.* New York: Harper Collins, 1997.

Chaikin, Andrew. *A Man On The Moon.* New York: Penguin Books, 1994.

Clark, Ronald. *Einstein – His Life And Times.* New York: Aron, 1993.

Englebert, Phyllis and Diane Dupris. *Handy Space Answer Book.* Detroit: Visible Ink, 1998.

Gralla, Preston. *How The Internet Works.* Indianapolis: Macmillian, 1998.

Harnack, Andrew and Eugene Kleppinger. *The Internet Guide For Students And Writers.* New York: St. Martin's Press, 1997.

Lowe, Janet. *Bill Gates Speaks.* New York: John Wiley And Sons, 1998.

OíHara, Shelley. *Netscape Beginner's Guide To The Internet.* Arizona: 1998.

Statistics And Data

Bernstein, Peter and Christopher Ma (eds.) *The Practical Guide To Practically Everything.* New York: Random House, 1997.

Carrier, Rhonda (ed.) *The Guinness Book Of World Records 1999.* New York: Guinness Publishing, 1998.

Covey, Sean. *7 Habits Of Highly Effective Teens.* New York: Fireside, 1998.

Reference Resources

Freedman, Michael. *Word Smart*. New York: Random House, 1997.

Freedson, Grace (ed.) *Barron's New Student's Concise Encyclopedia*. Barron's Press, 1993.

Lamm, Kathryn. *10,000 Ideas For Term Papers, Projects, Reports, And Speeches*. New York: Macmillian, 1998.

Lesko, Matthew. *Information USA*. New York: Penguin, 1986.

New York Public Library. *Desk Reference*. New York: Macmillan General Reference, 1998.

Panati, Charles. *Panati's Extraordinary Origins Of Everyday Things*. New York: Harper & Row, 1989.

Reed, Laura (ed.) *Webster's New World Pocket Book Of Facts*. New York: Simon & Schuster, 1998.

Thompson, Fiona and Kate Phelps. *The 20th Century Year By Year*. New York: Barnes & Noble, 1997.

About The Author

Stephen M. Gower, CSP, blends the theory of speech with professional speaking as few in the world can do. For more than a decade, Stephen taught public speaking on the college level as an adjunct professor. He has delivered more than four thousand speeches, and has earned the Certified Speaking Professional designation. The CSP is the highest earned designation presented by the National Speakers Association. Worldwide, less than 400 speakers have earned their CSP.

Mr. Gower received the Bachelor's Degree from Mercer University, and the Master's Degree from Emory University. He is also the author of *Celebrate The Butterflies – Presenting With Confidence In Public*. *The Missing Lynx* is Stephen's tenth book.

Mr. Gower speaks for youth groups across the country. For information on his availibility for your organization, call toll free - **1-800-242-7404.**

Quantity Discounts Available

Quantity discounts on *The Missing Lynx – Finally, A Speak-In-Public Learning System For High School Students* and/or *Celebrate The Butterflies – Presenting With Confidence In Public* are available.

Call toll free - 1-800-242-7404.

Stephen Speaks For Youth Groups

For more information on Keynote Speeches, Special Occasion Speeches, Seminars, Consulting, Books, and Tapes by Stephen M. Gower, CSP, and for other Gower Growth Systems Products and Services, contact:

The Gower Group, Inc.
P. O. Box 714, Toccoa, GA 30577
1-800-242-7404 Fax: 706-886-0465
E-Mail: smg@stephengower.com
Visit Our Web Site:
http://www.stephengower.com

Notes

Notes

Notes

Notes

Notes

Notes

Notes

Notes

Notes

Notes

Printed in the United States
75308LV00002B/1-180

9 781880 150566